DATE DUE

Grasshoppers

Trudi Strain Trueit

Cavendish
Square

New York

Published in 2014 by Cavendish Square Publishing, LLC
303 Park Avenue South, Suite 1247, New York, NY 10010

Library of Congress Cataloging-in-Publication Data

Trueit, Trudi Strain.
Grasshoppers / Trudi Strain Trueit.
p. cm. — (Backyard safari)
Summary: "Identify specific grasshoppers. Explore their behavior, life cycle, mating habits, geographical location, anatomy, enemies, and defenses"—Provided by publisher.
Includes bibliographical references and index.
ISBN 978-1-60870-246-6 (hardcover) • ISBN 978-1-62712-029-6 (paperback) • ISBN 978-1-60870-819-2 (ebook)
1. Grasshoppers—Juvenile literature. I. Title.
QL508.A2T776 2013
595.7' 26—dc23
2011032844

Editor: Christine Florie
Art Director: Anahid Hamparian
Series Designer: Alicia Mikles

Expert Reader: Alexandre V. Latchininsky, PhD, associate professor/extension entomologist, University of Wyoming, Laramie

Photo research by Marybeth Kavanagh

Cover photo by James Urbach/SuperStock
The photographs in this book are used by permission and through the courtesy of: *Alamy*: Florida Images, 4; A & J Visage, 6; Jeremy Pardoe, 14; Om Images, 16; Scott Camazine, 20, 22-3B; Juniors Bildarchiv, 22 (top); Rick & Nora Bowers, 22-2B; Arco Images GmbH, 22-2C; Premaphotos, 22-2D; All Canada Photos, 22-3A; Mike Briner, 22-3D; *Getty Images*: Harry Fox/Oxford Scientific, 7; *SuperStock*: age fotostock, 8L; Minden Pictures, 8R; James Urbach, 10, 23-1C; Animals Animals, 12; imagebroker.net, 15; NHPA, 23-1A, 28; *Media Bakery*: Veer, 13(net); BigStockPhoto, 13(cap), 13 (sunglasses); *Cutcaster*: Sergej Razvodovskij, 13(pencils); *Photo Researchers, Inc.*: Nature's Images, 22-2A; James H. Robinson, 23-1B; *Animals Animals-Earth Scenes*: Carroll W. Perkins, 22-3C; *AP Photo*: Mori Chen, 25; *Minden Pictures*: David Burton/FLPA, 26

Printed in the United States of America

Contents

Introduction

Have you ever watched baby spiders hatch from a silky egg sac? Or seen a butterfly sip nectar from a flower? If you have, you know how wonderful it is to discover nature for yourself. Each book in the Backyard Safari series takes you step-by-step on an easy outdoor adventure, then helps you identify the animals you've found. You'll also learn ways to attract, observe, and protect these valuable creatures. As you read, be on the lookout for the Safari Tips and Trek Talk facts sprinkled throughout the book. Ready? The fun starts just steps from your back door!

ONE
Leggy Leapers

You're walking barefoot through your yard when a leaf pops up out of the grass. Wait! Leaves can't jump. You've discovered a grasshopper.

Grasshoppers are among North America's most plentiful insects. They live in prairies, meadows, mountains, and deserts. You may even find them at the beach. Grasshoppers are also among the biggest insects on the North American continent. The largest measure about 3 inches long. Their abundance and size make grasshoppers perfect for a backyard safari.

A Hopper Grows Up

A grasshopper goes through three stages of growth: egg, **nymph**, and adult. In the summer or fall, adult grasshoppers lay their eggs a couple

Trek Talk
North America is home to more than six hundred different kinds of grasshoppers.

of inches down in the soil. Eggs are laid in batches called egg pods. Each egg pod may contain anywhere from a few eggs to more than one hundred. A female releases a foam to cover the eggs. The foam hardens, protecting the eggs from **predators** and cold weather. Grasshopper eggs remain in the soil during the winter and hatch the following spring.

A female grasshopper releases protective foam over its newly laid eggs.

The first nymph, or young grasshopper, to hatch digs to the surface. The other newborn nymphs follow. A nymph is the size of a grain of rice and looks like its parents, though it doesn't have wings. Some nymphs do not have their full colors, while others are quite colorful. Like all insects, grasshoppers have a hard outer covering called an **exoskeleton**. To grow, a nymph must **molt**, or shed this exoskeleton. It does this every one to two weeks by puffing up its body with air, splitting its exoskeleton, and wriggling free. With each molt, the grasshopper's wings grow and form, too. A nymph will molt five times before becoming an adult.

A growing grasshopper nymph molts its exoskeleton (right) a few times before reaching its adult size.

Most adult grasshoppers live for only a couple of months. Grasshoppers usually eat plants—and plenty of them. An adult grasshopper may eat its weight in plants every single day.

Grasshoppers Head to Tip

Grasshoppers belong to a group of insects called Orthoptera (awr-THOP-tuh-ruh). It's a Greek word meaning "straight winged." Locusts, crickets, and katydids also belong to this group. Most grasshoppers have two pairs of wings. The front wings help to hide and protect the hind flight wings.

Color Magic

Grasshoppers are masters of **camouflage**. They tend to come in various shades of green, brown, or gray to match the grass, leaves, rocks, and soil where they live. The desert grasshopper looks like sand! On the ground, such camouflage makes it difficult for birds, raccoons, snakes, and other predators to spot grasshoppers. However, in flight it's a different story. Many grasshoppers have hind wings that are yellow, orange, pink, red, or blue. These vivid colors help to attract a mate. Below the desert grasshopper (left) at rest blends into its surroundings and the blue-winged grasshopper (right) displays its colorful wings in flight.

A grasshopper has a head, thorax, and abdomen. The head features a pair of antennae, chewing mouthparts, and five eyes. Grasshoppers have two large compound eyes made up of thousands of tiny lenses. These multifaceted eyes allow the insect to see in every direction, even backward. Grasshoppers also have three tiny, single-lens eyes between the compound eyes. They help the grasshopper tell if it's day or night.

A grasshopper has six legs attached to its thorax. Despite their bouncy name, these insects prefer to walk using their short front and middle legs rather than jump with their powerful hind legs. Why? It takes a great deal of energy to make big leaps. Grasshoppers jump only when they have to.

Safari Tip
A grasshopper's antennae are usually less than half the length of its body. If you come across an insect that looks like a grasshopper with antennae longer than its body, it's probably a cricket or katydid.

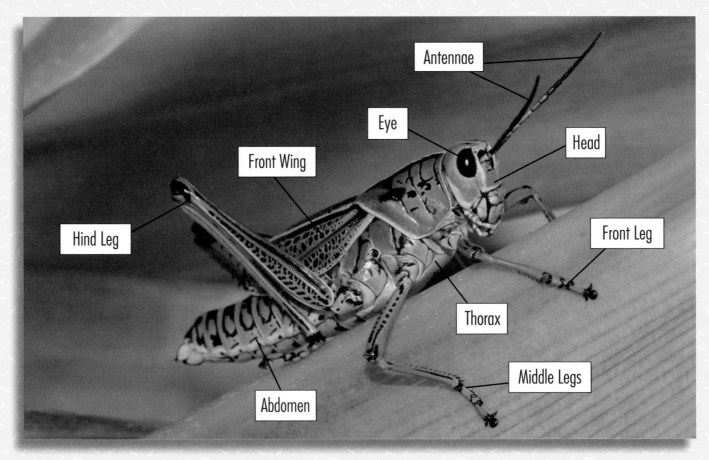

Antennae

Eye

Head

Front Wing

Front Leg

Hind Leg

Thorax

Middle Legs

Abdomen

Grasshoppers are insects related to katydids and crickets. They have chewing mouths, two pair of wings, and six legs.

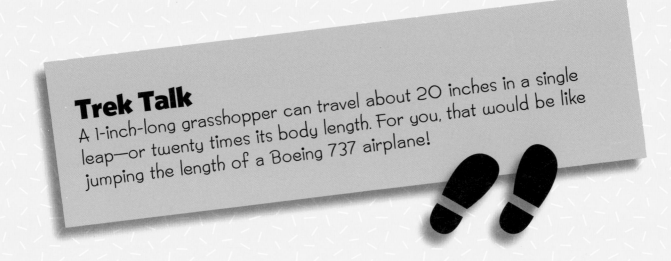

Trek Talk
A 1-inch-long grasshopper can travel about 20 inches in a single leap—or twenty times its body length. For you, that would be like jumping the length of a Boeing 737 airplane!

At rest, some grasshoppers make sounds by rubbing their hind legs against their front wings. This is called **stridulation** (stri-juh-LAY-shun). The noise sounds like buzzing, tapping, clicking, or low whistling. Some grasshoppers make sounds in flight. They use their wings to create a crackling noise. Scientists aren't completely sure how grasshoppers accomplish this. Such wing snapping is known as **crepitation** (kre-puh-TAY-shun). Male grasshoppers will stridulate or crepitate to call for a mate. Females have no trouble hearing male calling songs. Grasshoppers have a pair of eardrumlike structures called **tympana**. The tympana are located on the outside of the upper abdomen and are hidden by the wings. When it hears a male call, a female grasshopper will stridulate in return. Each type of grasshopper that sings has its own special calling song. But not all grasshoppers sing. Most of those in North America don't make noise. These grasshoppers find mates by sight or touch, or by releasing special chemicals called **pheromones** (FER-uh-moans). Now that you know more about the lives of grasshoppers it's time to find them for yourself. Are you ready? Let's safari!

TWO

You Are the Explorer

Grasshoppers can be found in most areas of North America from April to October. If you live in an area where temperatures usually stay above 50 degrees Fahrenheit, you can spot grasshoppers year-round.

Like butterflies, grasshoppers must **bask** before becoming active. They rest in the sun, warming their bodies for flight. Choose a warm, sunny day for your safari when the winds are calm. Grasshoppers will be basking on the stems of plants or on top of the dirt in the early morning and late afternoon. If you want to take photographs, these are the best times to go. If you'd rather see grasshoppers in action, head out from 11 a.m. to 3 p.m.

Trek Talk
At barely a half inch long, grasshoppers in the pygmy family are the smallest grasshoppers in North America.

What Do I Wear?

* A hat with a brim
* A long-sleeved shirt
* Jeans or long pants
* Sunglasses
* Sunscreen

What Do I Take?

* A pair of close-focusing binoculars (4 to 6 feet)
* Magnifying glass
* Small insect net (if you have one and want to try to catch a grasshopper for a closer look)
* A clear plastic container and a lid (poke six small holes in the lid)
* Digital camera
* Notebook
* Colored pens or pencils
* Water

Where Do I Go?

Grasshoppers will be attracted to these things in your backyard:

❅ Sunny, open, grassy areas

❅ Low-growing plants and shrubs

❅ Flowers

❅ Vegetables

❅ Dirt path

If your backyard doesn't offer these features, here are some other good safari locations:

❅ Public parks

❅ Open fields

❅ Meadows or pastures

❅ Woodlands

❅ Desert grasslands

Search for grasshoppers camouflaged to look like grass, leaves, or rocks.

Love Those Lubbers

Measuring up to 3 inches in length, lubbers are the largest grasshoppers in North America. The word *lubber* means "big and clumsy," and these insects live up to their name. Lubbers have short wings on their chubby bodies, so most cannot fly. Instead, they crawl awkwardly on the ground. Lubbers are also quite colorful. They often sport bright red wings with black-and-yellow bodies. Their flashy colors are a warning to predators that they are poisonous to eat. Lubbers can be found on leafy plants, such as sunflowers, lilies, and vegetables.

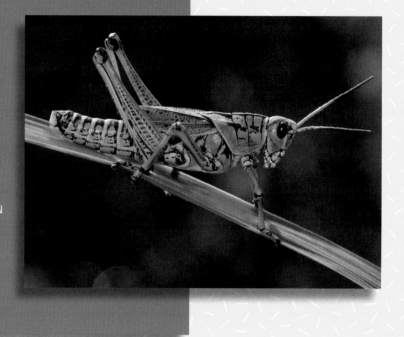

Always have an adult with you if you are going beyond your backyard. Be sure to stay on public property.

What Do I Do?

❊ Select a sunny, open spot to begin your safari. Use your binoculars to scan the area for grasshoppers. Look carefully! Grasshoppers easily blend in with dirt, grasses, and plants. Go in for a closer look with your magnifying glass. Search stems, leaves, twigs, and logs for grasshoppers that may be basking.

A cattail toothpick grasshopper looks like a tiny stick, stem, or blade of grass and can easily hide from its predators.

* Slowly and quietly, walk the area. Keep alert. Listen for any buzzing, tapping, or clicking sounds that last from ten to thirty seconds. You are likely to hear grasshoppers stridulating or crepitating before you see them.

* If you spot a grasshopper, keep your distance at first. Grasshoppers are easily spooked, so take a photo or make a quick sketch before moving in for a closer look.

* Make an entry in your notebook. Describe the grasshopper. Is it thin or fat? What color is its abdomen? Do you see any stripes, rings, or other **field markings**? Can you see the color of the insect's hind legs? How about its wings? Are they short or long? Also, note where you saw the grasshopper and what it was doing. Leave a blank line at the bottom to add the insect's name later.

GRASSHOPPER

Head: brownish-yellow, oval shaped,
   brown eyes, yellow antennae

Body: brownish-yellow with black stripes

Hind legs: yellow with black V-shaped
   markings

Wings: clear, shiny

Location/Activity: perched on weed stem
   near vegetable garden

Insect name: _____

Your Drawing or
Photo Goes Here

Safari Tip

Grasshoppers don't have stingers and usually won't bite (katydids and crickets, however, will bite). Still, you need to be careful if you are going to handle them. The sharp spines on the hind legs of some grasshoppers can cut skin. Also, some grasshoppers, such as lubbers, may hiss and spray a foul-smelling chemical when threatened. The brown liquid, nicknamed "tobacco spit" for its resemblance to tobacco juice, is meant to sicken small predators, such as spiders and birds. It shouldn't harm you.

* If you brought a net and a container, you may try to capture the grasshopper for a brief study. Gently place your net over the grasshopper. Place the container in the net and nudge the insect into it. Be gentle. Snap the lid onto the container.
* Keep the grasshopper for no more than ten minutes. Use your time to make more detailed notes and take more pictures or make another drawing. When the ten minutes are up, gently return the grasshopper to the spot where you found it.
* Spend about a half hour to an hour on safari (don't forget to drink your water).
* Clean up the area and take everything with you when you leave.

Congratulations on completing your grasshopper safari! Did you have fun? Don't worry if you didn't discover many grasshoppers. It can take a few tries to find these shy, well-camouflaged creatures. If you did find a grasshopper or two, you are ready to move on to the next chapter.

THREE
A Guide to Grasshoppers

You've had a busy day on the trail of grasshoppers. It's time to identify the insects you discovered. Here's what to do. Select an entry from your notebook. If you took a photo, print it and paste it next to its description. Take a good look at your notes and photo or sketch. As you compare your findings to the grasshoppers on the following pages, ask yourself these questions:

❋ What is the shape of the grasshopper's head? Is it round, oval, or cone shaped?

❋ What shape and color is the grasshopper's body? Does it have any field markings (spots or stripes)?

❋ Does the grasshopper have any unusual features, such as a crest on its thorax or a spike beneath its head?

❋ What color(s) are the hind legs?

❋ What shape, color, and size are the front wings (and hind wings, too, if you saw them)?

If you find a match, congratulations! Write the grasshopper's name in your notebook.

GRASSHOPPER

Head: brownish-yellow, oval shaped,
    brown eyes, yellow antennae

Body: brownish-yellow with black stripes

Hind legs: yellow with black V-shaped
    markings

Wings: clear, shiny

Location/Activity: perched on weed stem
    near vegetable garden

Insect name: differential grasshopper

Gras hopers are
esecre to find

If you can't make an exact match, you may still be able to tell which family your grasshopper belongs to. Compare it to these major groups, or families, of North American grasshoppers:

* **Stridulating Slant-faced:** cone-shaped head, slanted face, long slender body that is green or brown, hind wings that are not usually colorful
* **Band-winged:** oval or round head, thick body that tends to be either gray or brown and marked with dark spots, colorful hind wings that may have black bands
* **Spur-throated:** oval or round head, slanted face, small spike jutting out from under the head between the front legs, thin brown or green body with spots or stripes, clear hind wings (wings may have spots); most common grasshoppers in North America
* **Lubber:** oval head, body that is colorful and large (up to 3 inches in length), small wings
* **Pygmy:** smallest grasshopper (about half an inch in length), often brown with spots to blend in with dirt, leaves, and stones; found in damp places, such as near streams and ponds

Grasshopper Guide

STRIDULATING SLANT-FACED

Marsh Meadow Grasshopper

BAND-WINGED

Northern Green-Striped
Grasshopper

Red-Winged
Grasshopper

Carolina Grasshopper

Kiowa Grasshopper

SPUR-THROATED

Two-Striped
Grasshopper

Differential
Grasshopper

Red-Legged
Grasshopper

American Bird
Grasshopper

Grasshopper Guide

LUBBER

Plains Lubber
Grasshopper

Southeastern
Grasshopper

Eastern Lubber
Grasshopper

PYGMY

Black-Sided Pygmy
Grasshopper

FOUR

Try This!
Projects You Can Do

In ancient China the grasshopper was a symbol of good luck. It's no wonder that these insects were prized. Grasshoppers are important to our environment. They munch on unwanted weeds. Their droppings add valuable nutrients to the soil. However, hungry hoppers can cause problems, too. They often eat the corn, cotton, wheat, and other crops farmers are growing for humans. They also like to dine on the rangeland grasses being grown for cattle, horses, and other livestock. Many farmers considered them to be **pests**. Each year grasshoppers cause billions of dollars in rangeland and crop damage in North America. In places such as Asia and Africa, the destruction can be so extreme, it puts people at risk for starvation.

Locusts: Clouds of Trouble

Grasshoppers and their cousins, locusts, are eating machines. Locusts may **swarm**, or fly in large numbers, over long distances in search of food. During the mid-nineteenth century, about once every seven to twelve years a **plague** of Rocky Mountain locusts swept across North America eating everything in sight. Seeing fluttering clouds made up of millions of locusts terrified farmers and ranchers. They were helpless to stop the insects from dropping from the sky and devouring every single crop, leaf, and blade of grass in the fields. They ate shoes, fence posts, clothing, and even the fleece right off the sheep! In 1875 the largest recorded locust swarm in U.S. history—1,800 miles long and 100 miles wide—devastated the Great Plains. Yet by 1902 the Rocky Mountain locust was nowhere to be found. Scientists say it's likely that farmers plowing near the Rocky Mountains, where the grasshoppers laid their eggs, unknowingly helped wipe out the pest that had caused them such harm. Today there are no known locusts in North America; however, these insects continue to cause major crop damage in Africa, Asia, and the Middle East.

Scientists are studying grasshoppers to learn more about their feeding habits, behaviors, and abilities. You can observe grasshoppers, too, with the following projects.

Flower Garden

Plant a small flower garden to attract grasshoppers to your backyard. Choose six to eight plants from the list on page 27. Pick a sunny spot for your garden. Use good soil. Water your garden every morning in the summer. Never use pesticides. On a warm afternoon, count how many grasshoppers stop by the garden for a meal. Do your grasshoppers prefer one type of flower over another? Do they like the leaves or the blossoms best? Write down your observations in your notebook.

Plant a garden to attract grasshoppers to your backyard.

Plant List

marigold, lily, sunflower, cosmos, daisy, lavender, black-eyed Susan, zinnia, petunia, fountain grass

Taste Test

Some grasshoppers are extremely picky eaters, while others will feast on almost anything. Try this experiment to see which foods the grasshoppers in your yard like best. Find a 6-inch-by-6-inch (or larger) square plastic container and matching lid. Poke six holes in the lid. Gather these four items: several blades of grass, a fresh leaf from a plant, a dandelion, and a flower blossom. Put one food in each corner of the container. Carefully place a grasshopper inside the container and snap on the lid. Watch and wait for ten minutes. Did your grasshopper nibble on anything? What was its favorite food? Make an entry in your notebook jotting down the type of grasshopper you tested and what it ate. After ten minutes, carefully place the grasshopper back where you found it.

Jumping Course

How far can a grasshopper leap? To find out, you'll need a leaf, two pencils, a tape measure, and a friend. Find a grasshopper nymph that's resting on the ground (you can use an adult grasshopper, too, but it

Trek Talk

The great crested is a stunning grasshopper! It has a bulging crest behind its head, a vivid green body, and bright orange hind wings (the colorful hind wings are hidden by green forewings with brown spots and can only be seen while the insect is in flight). This beauty is found on the southern Great Plains, from Wyoming to Mexico and east to Kansas.

may fly away). Give your friend a pencil and have him/her stand 3 feet in front of the insect. To make the grasshopper jump, gently tap the hind end of its abdomen with your leaf. When it jumps, drop your pencil on the ground to mark its starting point. Your friend should place his/her pencil at the landing spot. Measure the distance between the pencils with your tape measure. How far did your hopper travel? Write it in your notebook. After two jumps, let your grasshopper go on its way.

Grasshoppers are plentiful from spring through fall so safari for them as often as you want. You might get lucky, like eleven-year-old Daniel Tate of England. He found a common green grasshopper that was bright pink! Scientists say such a quirk of nature is rare, but it does happen. Who knows what you'll discover on your backyard safari!

Glossary

bask	to soak up heat from the sun
camouflage	to use color as a disguise
crepitation	a grasshopper's way of producing sound through wing snapping
exoskeleton	the hard, protective outer covering of an insect
field markings	spots, bands, stripes, and other distinguishing marks on an animal
molt	the shedding of an exoskeleton
nymph	a young grasshopper
pests	destructive animals
pheromones	chemicals released by grasshoppers used for communication and mating
plague	a large group of millions of locusts that cause wide spread destruction
predators	animals that hunt other animals for food
stridulation	a grasshopper's way of producing sound by rubbing a hind leg against a front wing
swarm	a large group of insects that fly together
tympana	the external eardrumlike structures on a grasshopper

Find Out More

Books

Burris, Judy, and Wayne Richards. *The Secret Lives of Backyard Bugs*. North Adams, MA: Storey Publishing, 2011.

Nelson, Robin. *Grasshoppers*. Minneapolis, MN: Lerner, 2009.

Petrie, Kristin. *Grasshoppers*. Edina, MN: ABDO, 2009.

DVDs

Nova: Bugs. WGBH Boston Video, 2007.

Who Wants to Be an Entomologist? Victory Multimedia Consignment, 2009.

Websites

BioKIDS: Grasshoppers and Relatives

www.biokids.umich.edu/critters/Orthoptera

Discover more about how grasshoppers grow, eat, and communicate at this website developed by the University of Michigan. Click on the picture gallery for photos of common North American grasshoppers.

Bugfacts.net

www.bugfacts.net

Log on to this educational website to download an insect checklist to take with you on your safari. Have a question about grasshoppers? Click on *Ask a Scientist* to submit your question to an expert.

National Geographic: Grasshoppers

http://video.nationalgeographic.com/video/player/animals/bugs-animals/grasshoppers/

Watch a video of locusts swarming and discover what scientists are learning about their destructive, feeding-frenzy behavior.

Index

Page numbers in **boldface** are illustrations.

About the Author

TRUDI STRAIN TRUEIT often finds grasshoppers basking on (and munching) her flowers. A nature writer and photographer, she has authored more than seventy nonfiction books for children, including *Caterpillars and Butterflies*, *Dragonflies*, and *Birds* in the Backyard Safari series. Trueit is a former television weather forecaster and news reporter and has a BA in Broadcast Journalism from Pacific Lutheran University in Tacoma, Washington. She grew up in Seattle, Washington, and still lives in the Northwest with her husband, Bill, a high school photography teacher. Visit her website at www.truditrueit.com.

For every blue whale alive today
there were once twenty.
People hunted and killed so many of them
that fewer than 10,000 remain.
Now blue whales are protected
and hunting them is banned,
so in some places their numbers
are growing — very, very slowly.
Still, you could sail the oceans for a year
and never see a single one.

For Joseph and Gabriel
N. D.

For Dilys
N. M.

Text copyright © 1997 by Nicola Davies
Illustrations copyright © 1997 by Nick Maland

First U.S. edition 1997

Library of Congress Cataloging-in-Publication Data

Davies, Nicola.
Big blue whale / Nicola Davies ; illustrated by Nick Maland. —
1st U.S. ed.
Summary: Examines the physical characteristics, habits, and habitats
of the blue whale.
ISBN 1-56402-895-X (hardcover)
1. Blue whale—Juvenile literature. [1. Blue whale. 2. Whales.]
I. Maland, Nick, ill.   II. Title.
QL737.C424D38   1997
599.5'1—dc20   96-42327

10 9 8 7 6 5 4 3 2

Printed in Hong Kong

This book was typeset in Centaur.
The pictures were done in pen, ink, and wash.

Candlewick Press
2067 Massachusetts Avenue
Cambridge, Massachusetts 02140